Discover Sharks

GREAT WHITE
SHARK

Camilla de la Bédoyère

QEB
QEB Publishing

Copyright © QEB Publishing 2012
First published in the United States in 2012 by
QEB Publishing, Inc.
A Quarto Group Company
3 Wrigley, Suite A
Irvine, CA 92618

www.qed-publishing.co.uk

A CIP record for this book is available from the
Library of Congress.

ISBN 978 1 60992 400 3

Printed in China

Consultant Mary Lindeed
Editor Tasha Percy
Designer Melissa Alaverdy

Picture credits
Key: t = top, b = bottom,
m = middle, l = left, r = right

Getty Images Mike Parry/Minden Pictures 10-11
FLPA Mike Parry/Minden Pictures 6-7, Gerard Lacz 8-9,
Malcolm Schuyl 12-13, Mike Parry/Minden Pictures 14-15,
Stephen Belcher/Minden Pictures 18-19, Mike Parry/
Minden Pictures 22-23
NHPA Douglas David Seifert 1
OceanwideImages.com 4-5, 10br, 17tr
Photoshot TTL/Photoshot 16m, Eric Nathan 20-21
Shutterstock irabel8 2-3, Krzysztof Odziomek 16-17

Words in **bold**
are explained
in the Glossary
on page 24

CONTENTS

WHAT IS A GREAT WHITE?

A great white is a **shark**. It looks scary! It can swim very fast.

Look at those
enormous teeth.
Great white sharks
hunt animals to eat.

tooth

IS IT A FISH?

Yes, because all sharks are **fish**. Fish have **fins**. They breathe underwater.

Sharks use their **gills** to breathe.

fin

A great white has a dorsal fin on its back. It has a big fin at the end of its tail.

tail

SUPER SWIMMERS

Great white sharks are
super swimmers. They
have long, strong bodies.

A shark's body is a good shape for moving in water. Great whites are so strong they can leap out of the water.

HOW MANY TEETH?

Look at this shark's mouth. How many teeth can you see?

This tooth is from a great white shark. What shape is it?

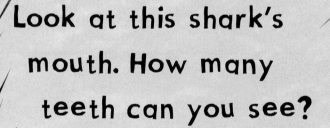

Real size!

When a tooth falls
out, a new one
takes its place.

OCEAN HOME

Great white sharks live in the oceans. They swim near the shore.

It is hard to see a
shark in the water.

The shark has a dark back.
It has a white belly.

FINDING FOOD

A great white shark swims silently in the ocean. It is looking for food to eat.

The shark has two
small black eyes.

The shark's
nose is called
a **snout**.

GOOD TO EAT

fish

The oceans are full of food for a hungry shark.

Great white sharks
like to eat fish,
dolphins, sea birds,
and other small
ocean **mammals**.

sea bird

dolphin

17

SHARK ATTACK

The shark can smell
a **seal**. Now it can
see a seal. It is
time to attack.

The shark grabs the seal
in its **jaws.** One gulp
and it's gone!

BIG BABIES

Great white sharks have babies every two or three years. Baby sharks are called **pups.**

A great white pup is about
51 inches (130 centimeters)
when it is born. It will
grow much bigger!

Now we know that great white sharks are amazing animals!

GLOSSARY

fin	a part on the body of a fish shaped like a flap, used for moving and steering through the water
fish	a cold-blooded animal that lives in water and has scales, fins, and gills
gill	the part of the body on a fish's side through which it breathes
jaws	the two bones in the face that hold the teeth
mammal	a warm-blooded animal with a backbone
pup	a young shark
seal	a sea mammal that lives in coastal waters and has thick fur and flippers
shark	a large and often fierce fish that feeds on meat and has very sharp teeth
snout	the long front part of an animal's head, including the nose, mouth, and jaws